Take up
Soccer

Take up Sport

Titles in this series currently available or shortly to be published:

Take up Soccer

Principal contributor:

Mike Smith

Mike Smith has managed teams in international matches on more than two hundred occasions; his current responsibility is the Welsh Youth Team

SPRINGFIELD BOOKS LIMITED

Copyright © Springfield Books Limited and White Line Press
1989

ISBN 0 947655 71 9

First published 1989 by
Springfield Books Limited
Springfield House, Norman Road, Denby Dale, Huddersfield
HD8 8TH

Edited, designed and produced by
White Line Press
60 Bradford Road, Stanningley, Leeds LS28 6EF

Editors: Noel Whittall and Philip Gardner
Design: Krystyna Hewitt
Diagrams: Barry Davies

Printed and bound in Great Britain

Photographic credits
Cover photograph: Associated Sports Photography
Colorsport: page 7
Noel Whittall: pages 11, 30, 42, 43, 54
All other photographs by **I. Arvid Parry Jones** (Aberystwyth)

Acknowledgements
Our thanks to the soccer players featured in most of the
photographs: Lee Brown, Martin Denham, Marc Hayes, Lee
Rogers, Robbie Savage, Ryan Wilson and other members of
the Welsh Under-16 Team; to the goalkeeper, Martin
Margettson; and to Merion Appleton at the Aberystwyth
Sports Centre.

Contents

Introduction

Surely *everybody* knows what soccer is all about? It's running after a ball and scoring goals, isn't it? Yes, goals are important in soccer, but you won't get them without quick thinking, agility, staying power and the ability to work with others. *Take up Soccer* introduces you to these skills, and will help you become a welcome member of a winning team.

This book deals mainly with the full game of soccer, played by teams of eleven. You will meet practice games using smaller numbers of players, but these are used to prepare for the full game. Five-a-side football, played indoors, has become very popular, but it calls for tactics which differ from those of soccer in a variety of ways.

At first sight the object in soccer is very simple: eleven of you try to propel a ball through a goal at the other end of a field without using your hands; eleven others try to stop you doing this, while at the same time they try to get the ball through a goal at your end of the field. It is this constant mixture of defence and attack which makes the game so interesting. Even if your side is doing well, you cannot afford to relax for a moment, and every player in a successful team must always be on the alert.

Play soccer according to the rules. Play it hard, but always play it fairly. Never forget that soccer is about having *fun*.

How the game started

For thousands of years people have enjoyed kicking a ball according to rules of some sort. The balls have been made from all sorts of materials — pigs' bladders, leather, rags or basketwork. Goals could be single posts, gates in walls or even the market crosses of neighbouring villages. Sometimes the pitch was a grassy field, but it was just as likely to be a muddy quagmire or the stone courtyard of a monastery.

Although the clothes and tactics have changed, these pre-war players would have no difficulty in recognising the skills of today's game.

Often the games developed into rough struggles, with many injuries. There was no single set of rules, and no opportunity for the players of one type of football to compete against others. Until the railways were built this did not matter much, as few people could afford to travel. However, by the middle of the nineteenth century, supporters of the types of football played in the British public schools were beginning to see that a common set of rules would allow fair matches between teams from different places. Before long, letters appeared in *The Times* which led to a historic meeting in London in 1863. This laid the foundation of the Football Association, but the rules which were eventually agreed were more like what we now know as rugby football. Handling the ball was allowed, and specialist goalkeepers had not yet been thought of.

It took fully another twenty years for most of the modern rules to be worked out, and for the name *soccer* to emerge — coined from the word *Association*.

No hands in soccer
Unless you are the goalkeeper, you cannot use your hands or arms to propel or control the ball at any time on the field of play. If you attempt this *deliberately*, the referee's whistle will blow for an offence. The referee will not penalise you for a genuinely accidental handling of the ball.

Although the principles of the game have not altered in the last hundred years, the style of play has changed. At first, it was a game where individual possession of the ball was important, and dribbling and dodging were the main features. Players stayed in fairly fixed positions unless they had the ball. When the effectiveness of passing the ball rapidly between members of the team became appreciated, play speeded up. As other countries, particularly those of central Europe and South America, took to the game, they introduced styles which have led to the current form of soccer. It is now a game in which the play should flow without too many stoppages, and in which all the players except the goalkeepers have to be equally ready to move forward on the attack or back to stop the other side scoring.

Soccer is now truly a worldwide sport. In spite of the efforts of the stupid few who make trouble, it is a powerful force for international goodwill. Air and coach travel enable amateur teams to make tours to other countries, and many young players make their first contacts with different cultures through the game.

Soccer is a game which is played with great enthusiasm by both sexes. Women's soccer is a fast-growing area of the sport. Throughout this book, "he" should be taken to apply equally to male or female players.

Stick to the rules

Cheats ruin the game for everybody, so don't be one! Soccer can be the finest game in the world, and it is our responsibility to keep it so.

Play fairly: obey the referee every time: know the rules: give credit for skilful play, regardless of team or nationality. Winning a hard-fought game will be a high point in your life, but winning at any cost will be nothing at all.

Figure 1 The pitch. The fixed dimensions are shown, but the overall size of the pitch can vary. ➡

2

The pitch and the players

The pitch

The pitch or *field of play* is marked out as shown in Figure 1. Ideally it should be of level grass, but players everywhere make do with almost any type of fairly level area. Quite a lot of variation in size is permitted too, although the minimum for international matches is 110 yd x 70 yd (100 m x 64 m) and the maximum 120 yd x 80 yd (110 m x 75 m). The length of a soccer pitch must always be greater than the width.

Ideally, the lines marking the sides of the pitch should be 2½ in to 3 in wide (65–75 mm). The goal-lines should be the same width as the depth of the goalposts, which must not be more than 5 in (125 mm). In soccer the ball remains in play until it has passed completely over the touchlines or goal-lines.

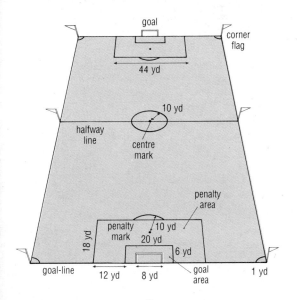

The players

A full team consists of eleven players, one of whom is the goalkeeper. You may play with fewer than eleven. Many practice games are played between teams of only five or six players, but these are not truly soccer, even though they call for most of the skills of the full-scale game.

Positions of the players

Each team will contain a number of *defensive* players, *midfield* players and *attacking* players. For many years it was usual for these to be very clearly defined, and each would cover a fairly small area of the pitch. As more and more countries have taken up the game, there have been experiments with different formations, and now it is often quite difficult to distinguish between positions. In the modern game it is common for almost all the players to go forwards on the attack and to run back into defence when necessary: only the goalkeepers stay in fairly fixed positions.

Figure 2 shows a typical formation of a team. This layout is referred to as 2-4-4, as there are two forwards or strikers, four midfield players and four backs. Modern football is very fluid, and you will meet other formations such as 4-2-4 and 4-3-3.

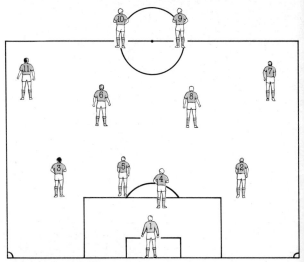

Figure 2 A typical 2-4-4 team formation: 1 goalkeeper, 2 right-back, 3 left-back, 4 and 5 centre-backs, 6 left-midfield, 7 outside-right, 8 right-midfield, 9 and 10 strikers, 11 outside-left

Officials

As well as the players, you need a *referee* and two *linesmen*. The referee has to enforce the laws of the game and see that play takes place for the correct lengths of time. Referees should carry a whistle and a notebook: the whistle is to start and stop play, and the notebook is for recording the names of players who commit serious deliberate offences, as well as for noting the time that the final whistle should be blown. It is recommended that referees carry a spare whistle too.

The *linesmen* have to judge when the ball has gone out of play by passing over the touchlines or goal-lines. They have to indicate this with their flags and show which team is entitled to the throw-in. They should also call the referee's attention to rough play. The linesmen should at all times assist the referee, but the referee cannot be overruled by them.

A good referee will do all he can to keep the game flowing. Here he signals "play on".

A linesman patrols each touchline.

3

Equipment

Boots

Although we still talk of football *boots*, soccer is now played in shoes which do not reach the ankle. These can be lightweight, but do buy real leather, as it gives better protection than anything else when kicking.

Your boots are the most important part of your kit. They must fit correctly, so take time to check them properly when you buy them. Boots which fit well make ball control easier, and will be comfortable for a whole match. You can't play well if your feet hurt or are blistered! Fit must be correct both in width and length. Too small, and your toes will be cramped: too large, and you will get blisters on your heels as your feet move up and down. On most boots the widest part of the sole is indicated by a coloured strip, grooves, or small metal studs.

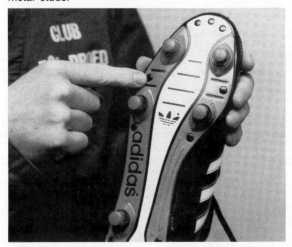

The widest part of the boot can easily be seen on the sole.

The ball of your foot must coincide with this part of the boot, or the fit will never be right. Before making your choice, try on boots from different manufacturers, taking the trouble to lace them up correctly and to *stand up* in them.

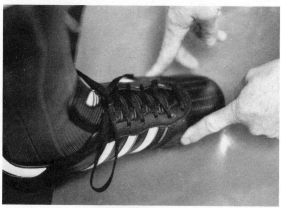

Check here...

...and here for a perfect fit.

When buying boots for growing youngsters, you have to strike a balance between allowing room for growth and the need for a snug fit for good ball control. Children's feet can easily be damaged by boots which are too tight, so fitting is extra important. Wearing a second pair of socks inside slightly large boots can help, but you have to accept that keen young players will need new ones quite often. It is quite wrong to try to play in boots as big as those in the top photo on page 14. Here the ball of the foot is too far behind the widest part of the sole: lasting out the game will be an effort in these, let alone winning!

These boots are simply too big — they will give the player problems, regardless of how many pairs of socks he uses.

You can lace the boots neatly in the normal manner, or tie the ends around the instep, which gives slightly more snugness.

The studs and bars on the sole of the boot must conform to international standards. Resilient rubber or plastic studs which are moulded into the boot may be $\frac{3}{8}$ in (10 mm) in diameter, provided that there are at least ten per boot. Where there are fewer than ten studs, they must be at least $\frac{1}{2}$ in (13 mm) in diameter.

Studs and bars must all be less than $\frac{3}{4}$ in (19 mm) deep.

It is the responsibility of the player to ensure that studs are fixed firmly and in good condition, with no sharp edges.

Training shoes

For much of your training, you will not want to use fully-studded match boots, so choose a good pair of trainers. Fit is still very important, but you have a wide choice of style. Do get trainers with leather uppers, which are much better for kicking, and make sure that the soles have a deep tread which will give a good grip on any surface.

Clothing

Football strip in the colours of a favourite team is a popular birthday or Christmas present. These are fine for practice and training, but not ideal for playing unless all your friends have similar kit. You need to be able to identify one of your own team at a glance so that you can pass the ball accurately when under pressure.

Goalkeepers need to take extra care with their kit. Padded clothing which protects the hips, shoulders and elbows is well worthwhile. Goalies stand still much more than other players, so a tracksuit top or extra sweater is essential in cold weather.

The stud at top right is dangerous, and would not pass a referee's inspection.

15

Goalkeepers need gloves which give a confident grip: padded jerseys are increasingly popular too.

It is usual for goalkeepers to wear gloves, and there are many types available which have palms and fingers specially designed to give a very positive grip on the ball. Don't fall into the trap of buying the biggest possible pair of gloves — if they are loose on your hands, you will be more likely to fumble the ball.

Wear socks made of wool or cotton. The type with a looped pile are particularly comfortable. Avoid nylon or other synthetics: they are not absorbent, and also become very hot through friction if you play on Astroturf or other plastic surfaces.

Do not wear anything which may injure either you or another player. This includes watches, bracelets or even earrings.

For training sessions, and for keeping warm before and after play, a tracksuit is a good investment.

Shin guards

FIFA, the governing body of world football, insists that shin pads are worn by all players in official matches, and this is good practice for everyone. In soccer you are bound to get bangs and scrapes on your legs, and shin guards will save a lot of pain and bruises.

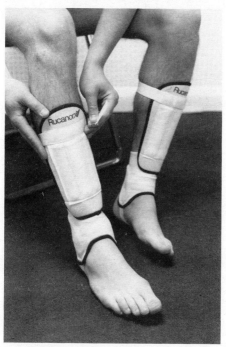

Shin guards are a must for match play: choose a pair which are light and comfortable.

The ball

Although a football will be provided at matches, you will be able to learn ball skills more quickly if you have your own to practise with. All official matches have to be played with a standard ball, but footballs do come in several other sizes too, and young players will progress more readily if they practise with a slightly smaller ball.

The requirements for a standard match ball are:

- It must be spherical, and cased in leather or an approved substitute.

- The circumference must be between 27 and 28 in (680–710 mm).

- The weight at the start of the match must be between 14 and 16 oz (396–453 g). This may change as the game progresses and the ball picks up water and mud; this was more of a problem with the all-leather balls of the past: modern footballs have a waterproof surface.

- The inflation pressure must be between 0.6 and 1.1 bar (8.5–15.6 lb/in^2).

4

The terms of the game

You will probably be familiar with most of the terms used in soccer, but there may be others which need to be explained fully. Here are the ones you need to know:

Corner

If a defender is the last player to touch the ball before it passes out of play behind the goal-line, without having gone through the goal, a corner kick (corner) is awarded. The kick is taken by a player from the attacking side, from the marked area next to the corner flag. The flag must not be removed when the kick is taken, and the ball must be completely within the marked area.

Corners give a valuable opportunity to score, because the attackers have time to position their players in front of the goal and can send the ball accurately to them. Goals can also be scored direct from a corner, and some players have become very skilled at kicking the ball so that it takes a curved flight into the goal.

Dropped ball

When play stops for a reason not directly due to the action of either team, the referee restarts the game by dropping the ball. This is done where the ball was when play was stopped, unless this was in the goal area, in which case it is dropped onto the front line of the goal area, at the nearest point to where it was when play stopped. The ball is not considered to be *in play* until it touches the ground, and it is an offence to try to play it while it is still in the air.

Typical reasons for using the dropped ball include restarting after the original ball has punctured, or after a stoppage for injury which was not caused by foul play.

Foul

A degree of physical contact is part of football, but there are very strict limits on what is allowed. If you tackle in a way which may injure another player, you commit a foul. Typical examples include tackling between the player's legs, so that he is tripped; tackling late, after he has

18

Re-starting play by means of a dropped ball. The ball is not in play until it touches the ground.

passed the ball, so that you bring him down; or charging another player in the back. There are dozens of other ways of committing a foul, such as handling the ball, and too many players accept them as a matter of routine. A good referee will be strict when penalising fouls.

Free kick

Free kicks are taken by the non-offending side to restart play after an offence. There are three types: *indirect*, *direct* and *penalty*.

In an *indirect free kick*, the ball must be played by, or at least touch, another player before a goal can be scored. Typical offences which are liable to result in an indirect free kick for the other side are:

● Dangerous play — for example, attempting to kick a ball which another player might reasonably be trying to head

● Deliberately obstructing an opponent who is in possession of the ball

● Attempting to gain ground by taking a throw-in at the wrong point after having been warned previously

● Improperly charging the goalkeeper

● Deliberate time-wasting by a goalkeeper in possession of the ball.

A *direct free kick* is given against more serious offences. As the name suggests, you are allowed to score without the ball touching any other player. Direct free kicks are awarded against the following nine offences; the first eight have to be deliberately committed on an opponent.

- Charging violently or dangerously
- Charging from behind, unless the opponent is obstructing
- Holding
- Pushing
- Striking, spitting or swinging at an opponent
- Kicking or attempting to kick an opponent
- Tripping
- Jumping at a player
- Deliberately handling the ball, other than by the goalkeeper within his own penalty area.

A *penalty kick* is awarded if the direct free kick offences above are committed within either of the *penalty areas* by a member of the attacking team. The offences must have been committed *deliberately*, in the opinion of the referee. The kick is taken from the *penalty spot*, which is 12 yards (11 metres) from the centre of the goal-line. The goalkeeper must stand behind the goal-line, between the goalposts, and is not allowed to move until the ball has been kicked. A goal can be scored directly from a penalty kick, but the kicker is not allowed to play the ball a second time until it has been touched by another player.

A penalty seen from behind the goal. Note how the goalie stays put until the ball has been kicked.

While a penalty kick is being taken, all the players other than the kicker and the goalkeeper must remain on the pitch, but outside the penalty area.

In play

There are several ways of starting or restarting play, including a free kick or a kick-off, but in all cases the ball has to travel a distance equal to its own circumference before being considered to be *in play*. You can check this distance by rolling a ball for one revolution: you will find that it covers about 27 in (680 mm).

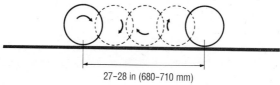

27–28 in (680–710 mm)

Figure 3 The ball must travel a distance equal to its circumference to be in play.

The ball remains in play throughout the match until it passes completely over the goal-line or touchline, or until the referee stops play. So always *play on until you hear the whistle* – even if you think an offence has been committed.

Marking

Marking is the skill of knowing where opposing players are, and allowing them as little space as possible by maintaining a position where you can intercept passes.

Offside

Soccer's offside rules are quite simple, yet they are often the cause of much argument! Basically the rules are:

● You will be in an offside position if you are in your opponents' half and nearer to the goal-line than the ball, *unless* there are two opponents nearer to the goal-line than you are. One of these can be the goal-keeper.

● Although you may be in an offside *position*, you will not be penalised for that alone unless you attempt to play the ball, obstruct an opponent, or otherwise take advantage of your position.

● If you are in an offside position, you will become truly offside at the moment one of your team passes the ball to you – not at the moment you receive it. However, if you run forward to take a pass from another member of your team, provided that you were not offside when it was kicked, you will not become offside during the passage of the ball.

21

● If the referee declares you to be offside, an *indirect free kick* is awarded to the other side. This is taken at the point where the offside occurred, unless you were in your opponents' goal area: in that case, they can take the kick from anywhere in the half of the goal area in which the offence occurred.

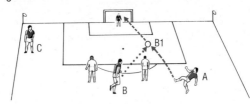

Figure 4 An offside example: A has the ball and kicks it to B1; B runs forward to take the ball at B1, and scores. C is on the far side of the field, standing still. Will the goal be allowed? Let's look at each player in turn:

A is not offside, because there are at least two defenders (three in this case) between him and the goal-line.

B is not offside either, because there were at least two defenders between him and the goal-line *at the moment* when A passed the ball forward.

C is in an *offside position*, but he will not be penalised for this, as it is unlikely that any referee would consider him to be taking part in the play or gaining any advantage from his position.

The goal will be allowed!

Tackle

You can take possession of the ball by tackling with your feet. Any attempt to tackle the player rather than the ball is a foul.

Ryan (dark strip) comes in to tackle Lee: Ryan makes firm contact with the ball, but note how Lee bends his knees to keep stable while resisting the challenge.

Throw-in

This is the method used to restart the game after the ball has been played over the touchline. The ball is thrown by a member of the team which did not last touch the ball. The thrower must face the pitch and deliver the ball from behind the head, using both hands; part of each foot must be on the ground as the ball is released. The ball has to be clearly *thrown*; it may not just be dropped.

The ball must be touched by another player before the thrower can again play it.

The ball becomes *in play* as soon as it crosses the touchline, but a goal cannot be scored directly from the throw — at least one other player must touch it first.

Players cannot be *offside* directly from the throw, either.

Below left: *Throwing in — the "ready" position: ball behind head, hands each side of the ball, and knees bent.*

Above right: *The throw — legs, body and arms work in sequence to release the ball with a whip-like action for maximum distance. Don't just throw for distance, though — make sure that you target a team-mate.*

Wall

When a free kick is being taken which is within shooting range of the goal, the defending players will usually form a wall by standing close together between the ball and the goal. The defenders have to be at least ten yards (9.15 m) from the kicker.

5

Playing the game

Scoring

The only way to score in soccer is by getting a goal. To do this the ball must pass completely over your opponents' goal-line, within the space limited by the goalposts and crossbar.

> **Goal or no-goal?**
> For a goal to be allowed, the following rules apply:
>
> ● The player attempting to score must be onside (not offside).
>
> ● If an *attacker* was the last player to touch the ball, it must not have been with the hand or arm. The only exception to this would be if a goal-keeper managed to throw the ball from his own penalty area into the opposing goal — hardly a common way of scoring!
>
> ● If a *defender* handles the ball, and it then passes into the goal, the goal is allowed.
>
> ● *All* of the ball must be over *all* of the line. However, it does not matter if it touches the posts or crossbar on the way in, or whether it bounces inside the goal and then out again. If this leads to discussion or dispute, then the referee's decision is final, as always.

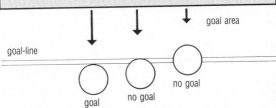

Figure 5 The ball must be *completely* behind the goal-line for the goal to count.

Period of play

A full game of soccer consists of two 45-minute playing periods, separated by a five-minute interval. The teams change halves after the interval. The referee can add time to the playing periods to make up for that lost owing to injury or accident.

Soccer matches for school, youth and women's teams may be of shorter duration, but the period has to be agreed before the start of the match.

Starting play

The two captains toss a coin to decide which team will kick off. The winner of the toss can choose either to kick off or to defend a particular goal. If you find yourself having to make this choice, do think about it: for example, your team may stand a better chance if you decide to play against the wind during the first half, when they are still fresh.

The game starts with a place kick from the centre of the halfway line. It is customary for the centre-forward to take the kick, but there is no rule about this. The ball must be kicked forwards into the opposing team's half of the pitch for a distance at least equal to its circumference (about 27 in, or 680 mm) — see page 21.

The team kicking off must all be on their side of the halfway line as the kick is made, and the opposition must be at least ten yards (9.15 m) from the ball. The centre circle indicates the ten-yard distance.

The player who kicks off is not allowed to play the ball a second time until another player has touched it. Before this rule was introduced, it was quite common for the ball to be dribbled all the way to the opposing goal by the player who took the kick-off. Similar rules which bar the player involved from playing the ball twice in succession apply to free kicks and throw-ins.

Play continues until the ball goes out of play by passing over the touchlines or goal-lines; until a goal is scored; or until the referee stops play — usually because an offence has been committed.

In games where a result other than a draw is needed — to decide a championship, for example — the teams may agree in advance to play *extra time* if the score is level at the end of the second half. This takes the form of an extra half-hour of play, with a change of ends after fifteen minutes. If the scores are still level after extra time, a *penalty shoot-out* can take place. Here five different players from each side take turns to try and beat the opposing goalkeeper from a penalty spot.

Possession

To score a goal, your team needs to be in possession of the ball. You are allowed to challenge a player who has the ball by *tackling* or by *charging*. Both these actions have to be performed fairly. The tackle must be directly at the ball — not at the player. If you charge the player who has possession, it must be shoulder to shoulder.

You can increase your chances of keeping possession by practising the skills of ball control. Learn to juggle the ball with your feet, knees, chest and head. This will give you confidence that you will be able to control it properly when it is passed to you. Learn to dribble, too, and to kick with either foot.

Passing and position

Passing and position are the keys to good football. It doesn't matter how brilliant your individual players are, if they don't get the ball, your team won't be able to score! An effective team is one which makes the best use of space by passing the ball to unmarked players. At the same time the opposition must be kept as tightly marked as possible.

As Lee moves in to tackle, Ryan (dark strip) has moved over. This just gives Robbie the angle he needs to make the pass.

In soccer, as in all ball games, you have to look at the ball to play effectively. Good positioning will ensure that you can keep your eye on it as much as possible.

As with shooting, accuracy is much more important than power when it comes to passing. You will find that you have the best control if you pass with the side of your foot, and keep the ball on the ground. This is also the easiest type of pass for your team-mate to receive.

Angles

Footballers often refer to the *angles* of play. The angle at which the ball comes to you can make all the difference between whether it is easy to play and pass on, or whether it is almost impossible.

A ball which comes to you from the direction you are facing is easy to see and control — particularly if you pass it on through a narrow angle. This is because you have it fully in view all the time, and the direction of your pass depends on a simple kick with the side of your foot.

Now imagine that you are standing in the same position, but the ball is passed from somewhere behind you. Because you cannot have your eyes fully on the ball, you will find it harder to receive it accurately. Your problems don't end there: the footwork needed to pass it on is more complicated than in the first example, yet you have less time to do it in.

Of course, you cannot always control the angle at which the ball comes, but some intelligent positioning can make a big difference quite often. Always be on the look-out for times when a move of a few metres or a change of direction can make the angle much more favourable for you.

Goalkeepers constantly calculate the angles when an attack is under way, and try to get into a position which gives the attackers the smallest possible choice of angle through which to shoot.

Figure 6 It is easy to pass the ball through a narrow angle (dashed line) within your uninterrupted field of vision (tinted area), because it is in view all the time: you know exactly what is going on. The wide-angled ball (solid line) presents more problems: if you simply watch the ball coming towards you, you lose touch with the action on your other side.

27

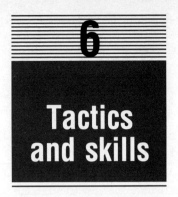

6

Tactics and skills

Whether you are having a kick-around with a few friends or taking part in a full match, you will play better if you have learned how important tactics are in soccer.

Tactics

You can practise tactical play even if you are only playing on a small pitch with five or six players a side. You will find that in the full-size game there are rarely more than half-a-dozen players around the ball at any time, so the tactics you learn in the smaller games will immediately be useful.

Tactics can be divided into three types:

● *overall tactics*
● *on-the-ball tactics*
● *off-the-ball tactics*.

Overall tactics

● **Football is played in triangles**
Watch a good team in action, noticing the pattern the ball follows as it is passed from player to player. You will see that it normally travels in triangles — sometimes big open triangles, sometimes small tight ones.

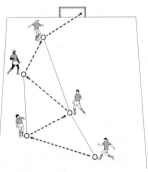

Figure 7 Triangles of play

- **Effective passes tend to be forwards and backwards**
  Passes directly to a player on one side or the other of you are very easily intercepted by the opposition. Passes forwards or backwards are harder to "read", and increase your chances of success.

On-the-ball tactics

- **Each player you beat increases the odds in favour of your team**
  You must develop the skill to handle challenges when you have the ball, and also appreciate that each opponent you pass increases the odds in your favour. Each time you beat another player, you have several new choices: do you retain the ball and meet the next challenge? do you pass forward to the left, or back and to the right? *You* must decide!

Off-the-ball tactics

Position
- Remember, position is everything. When your team has the ball, always try to be in a position where you will be an effective point of a triangle. Support the player with the ball by being where you can be seen, and try to think one step ahead, so that if the ball is passed to you, you will know what you are going to do with it!

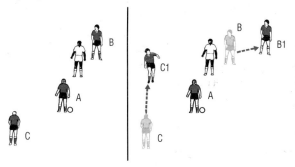

Figure 8 *Left:* A has the ball and a problem: he can't play to B, who is marked by an opponent, and he can't play to C, who is too far back for him to see.
Right: If A's team-mates see the problem developing and move to avoid it (B to B1, C to C1), A can see them both, and can choose which to play to.

- If the other team has possession, be aware of the *angles* the player with the ball needs to make a safe pass, and try to position yourself to stop the pass.

The teams arrange themselves at the goal-mouth in readiness for a corner kick. The three attackers on the right are marked by only one opponent, but the defender in the foreground (striped shirt) has seen this weakness and is going across to cover it.

Marking

Marking the opposition effectively makes all the difference when your team does not have possession of the ball. It doesn't matter whether you are playing a practice game with only five or six players each side, or the full game with eleven — the principle is the same: *mark one opponent*. If you mark a single player effectively, you make him valueless to the other side. Each player marked like this is one less who can spring an attack, and a single effective tackle can put your team back in control.

If in doubt about the best position to be in to mark a particular player, try to mark on the *inside*.

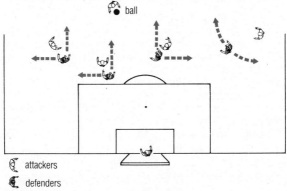

ℰ attackers

ℰ defenders

Figure 9 Try to mark on the inside.

Defence or attack?

Although the soccer pitch is divided into halves by the halfway line, you will find it easier to work out what to do at any stage of the game if you imagine it divided into thirds (see Figure 10).

30

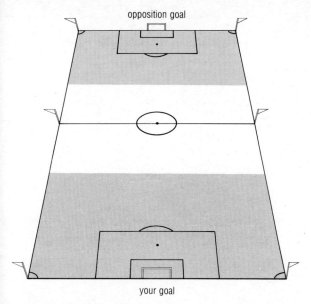

opposition goal

your goal

Figure 10 To help decide what to do, imagine the pitch divided into three roughly equal parts: the defence area (grey), midfield area (white) and attack area (blue).

The third of the pitch closest to your goal is the *defence area*, and here you should be playing careful short passes to prepare for a long pass (a *long ball*) to a team-mate in the midfield area.

In the *midfield area* there is more space you can make use of safely, and here you should form the over-all moves which will lead to a final strike at goal. This is where the groundwork is prepared to set up thrusts towards the goal, and great players do some of their best work here.

The *attack area* is the third in front of your oppo-nents' goal. Here's where the chance of getting a shot in must always be foremost in your mind, even though the defenders should not allow you much space in which to work. Keep the ball moving across in front of the goal, so that even if you are unable to get the angle right for a successful shot, one of your team-mates may get the opportunity.

Skills in attack

Beating each challenge

When you have the ball, each opponent you can get past increases the odds in favour of your team. Meet each challenge with confidence — decide whether to dodge, dribble or pass, then go for it in a positive way!

Robbie beats a defender. Keeping close to the ball as he dribbles, he changes from the inside of his foot to the outside as he sneaks the ball past Marc.

Moving up

Move the ball up the field fast, but always keep an eye on the offside situation — remember there have to be at least two opponents between you and the goal at the moment the ball is passed to you. Encourage your team to move up in full support of every attack.

Shooting

It is no good being able to gain possession and control the ball if you cannot score goals when the opportunity is there. Some players just can't shoot — they waste so much time deciding what to do that they never score! Make sure that you are not one of these. Here are some tips for getting the ball past the goalie:

● The further you are to the side of the goal, the easier it is for the goalkeeper to predict the angle at which the ball will be coming towards him. Shots from directly in front are the best for you, because you can pick any part of the goal-mouth to aim at.

● Run fast, and shoot as soon as you can: this won't give the goalkeeper time to sort out the angles (see page 27).

- Don't try to kick *too* hard: by all means hammer the goal home if the way is really clear, but remember that accuracy beats force every time! If in doubt, *shoot soft*, but make the ball go just where you want it. Too many shots go over the bar because the attacker struck too hard.

- If you cannot see a part of the goal which is undefended, send your shot low and close to the goalkeeper's legs. The goalie won't be able to get his hands to it easily, and even if he does manage to get a leg or foot to it, he still won't be able to make a controlled save. There is a fair chance that you or one of your team-mates will get a second shot.

- Shoot diagonally if you can. This is called "shooting across the goalkeeper", and makes his job more difficult.

- If you don't shoot, you won't score. You will not get the ball into the goal every time — two out of ten would be good going — but each shot increases your chances.

Keep up the pressure

If a shot misses, or is intercepted by the defence, don't give up the attack. Goals often come from a secondary attack after the main one has failed.

Skills in defence

If your team has lost possession of the ball, you must all work together to get it back. It really is a team job, in which effective marking plays a vital part. Here are some useful tips:

- Get back between the ball and your goal immediately, and *mark your opponent*.

- Maintain concentration. It is all too easy to let your mind think about other things when your team isn't getting the ball very often. It is no good finding suddenly that you have possession, but have lost touch with where your team-mates are.

- It is also easy to lose concentration by getting agitated about a foul which you imagine has been committed but which the referee has ignored. You can't do anything about it, so get on with the game and keep your mind on the job. Referees will take no notice of players who argue, so don't waste your time and mental energy in this way.

- The easiest way of getting the ball is by intercepting a pass, so think positionally all the time.

- Keep challenging the player in possession: don't let him have an easy time.

- Don't let the other side have space. Keep the pressure on through close marking.

- Defend the line to your goal. Figure 11 shows how play flows towards each goal. In the midfield area, almost the whole width of the pitch has to be covered, but the area narrows down as you get nearer to the goals. If the defenders draw in towards the middle of the pitch as they go back with the play, they have a better chance of intercepting a shot at goal.

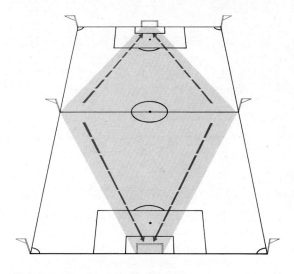

Figure 11 Play flows towards each goal.

- Tackle positively. It helps if you are big and fit, but smaller players can tackle very successfully too. Go in for the ball as if there is no doubt whatever that you will get it, and you will find that you usually do...

- If your team has given a free kick away within striking distance of your goal, learn how to set up a defensive wall of players standing shoulder-to-shoulder. Take care when doing this — listen to the instructions of your own goalkeeper who will tell you how many players to put in the wall. Do just as he says, and remember that he will probably not be able to see the kicker. If you have been part of a wall, make sure to get fully into the game again as soon as the ball is back in play — there is a tendency to relax for a moment when the shot has been saved and so to let the other side keep up the attack.

Ball-control skills

Trapping the ball

It is no good getting to the ball if you cannot control it when you have it! You need to learn how to deal with balls which come to you from all sorts of different heights and angles.

Lee lines up to trap the ball with the inside of his foot...

...he cushions it and brings it to the ground completely under control.

The main trick to learn is how to provide a slight cushioning effect, so that the ball seems to fall dead in front of you. Practise this by repeatedly kicking a ball against a wall and trapping it on the rebound. Keep on trying until you can "kill" it with your head, chest, thighs, knees and feet. Then go on until you can control the ball with the insides and outsides of both feet.

Using the bottom of your foot is also an important way of killing the ball. Just trap it as it bounces, with the toe of your boot higher than the heel. Then slide the foot to the side ready to pass or dribble at once. When using the underfoot trap, you must let the ball come quite close, so that you do not have to stretch forward with the trapping foot. If you do have to reach too far forward, you will tend to step onto the ball, which will make it very difficult to control your next move.

Once you are able to gather the ball up safely every time, you will find that your confidence on the field will increase very rapidly. Your team-mates will also become much more likely to send the ball to you.

Juggling

Juggling is an advanced type of ball control. It is also great fun to practise, and builds overall agility and fitness. Simply try to keep the ball in the air for as long as possible without touching it with your hands or letting it bounce on the ground. You can use your head, chest, thighs, knees, ankles and feet, but keep your hands out of the way!

You can vary this practice by juggling the ball against a wall, or by passing it to a friend — allowing only one bounce between the two of you.

You will not find time to juggle the ball for any length of time during a match, but the instinctive skills acquired will be extremely useful.

Dribbling

A good dribble means keeping the ball with you *and under control* as you take it past the defenders. Use both sides of your foot to coax the ball along, and slow it down with a touch of the sole on top of it. Dribbling is not just a matter of speed alone — you have to be able to change speed and direction at will. No matter how good you become in practice, when you get into a match you will find that the opposition will not allow you many chances to dribble. You can improve your chances by keeping your head up and positioning your body between the ball and your challenger whenever possible.

Dribbling practice: all the players are keeping really close to the ball.

Running with the ball

It sounds simple — yet this is one of the most important skills to master. You need to judge just how far ahead to nudge the ball so that you cover the open spaces fast and safely. You have to kick it far enough to let you keep up a good running speed, yet be able to bring it back fully under control if it looks as if you will have to dribble it past a challenger.

Heading the ball

If you learn to play the ball confidently with your head, you will give yourself an advantage over many players. There's no great secret: the usual rule of looking at the ball applies, and try to keep your eyes open as your head meets it. The ball should hit your forehead — *not* the top of your skull. You should always aim to head with a purpose, either to pass or to shoot.

Heading is best practised in pairs. It is not at all easy to keep your eyes open as you contact the ball!

Try some heading practice against a wall.

Practise by heading the ball against a wall: if you can, mix headed shots in with kicked ones, and keep the ball in play for as long as possible. Practise shallow-angle deflection shots with a couple of your friends. Stand between them, while they kick the ball to each other. They should try to send the ball past you above chest-height, while you try to deflect it using your head only.

From the start, try to get used to the idea that you head the ball with a purpose. Too many young players are content just to contact the ball, and do not try to make their headed shots *useful*.

Making the ball "bend" in flight

If you kick the ball so that it spins as it leaves your foot, you can make it curve through the air in flight. The main types of spin used are *sidespin* and *backspin*.

Sidespin is achieved by kicking low on the side of the ball as you see it (see Figure 12). You complete the kick with a smooth follow-through. The ball will tend to travel in a curve in the direction it is spinning. The main use for this kick is to bend the ball around the end of a defensive wall in front of a goal, but it can also be used to keep a pass clear of a defender. You will need lots of practice before you are able to make the ball curve accurately to where you want it.

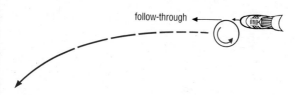

follow-through

Figure 12 To make the ball curve in flight, apply sidespin by kicking low on the side of the ball and following through smoothly.

Backspin is used in the chip shot. Your foot meets the ball as low as possible, and there is no follow-through. The idea is to make the ball rise steeply and then to fall fairly "dead" to the ground. If you hit the ball a fraction too high, or if you follow through at all, it will simply rise up at a relatively shallow angle, without much spin. The knack of hitting the ball with just the right combination of strength and speed is difficult to learn, but if you can master it, you may one day score by chipping the goal over a defensive wall and under the crossbar.

If the ball is rolling towards you, the chip becomes easier. You will quite often find that you can chip it back over the heads of opponents who have let it get a little too far ahead of them.

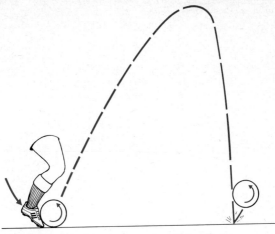

Figure 13 The chip shot — a low kick with no follow-through

Goalkeeping skills

Goalkeeping is a specialised job, which calls for the following:

● A supple body with good stretching ability

● Natural agility

● Good use of the hands. As the photographs show, there are two main positions for your hands, one to intercept low shots, and another for high ones. Always use two hands if you possibly can. Concentrate on getting the ball completely under control and pulling it towards your body for safety. It's no use getting to the ball if you cannot hang on to it most of the time.

The safe way to gather low- and medium-height shots

Use both hands for high shots too, whenever possible.

● The ability to dive and land safely. A good goalie will be able to avoid injury by not landing on the knee, hip or elbow joints, yet will still be able to throw himself full-stretch across the goal-mouth.

● The ability to *read* an attack. Correct anticipation is as important as fast reaction.

● You need a powerful kick to clear the ball away from the goal-mouth. A good goalkeeper will be able to kick to the halfway line in most conditions. If it is done powerfully and accurately, this clearance can be the first stage in building an attack on the other goal.

Courage, as well as a little padding, is an essential part of the goalkeeper's equipment.

- The goalkeeper's game is related to *angles* all the time. You must be able to calculate these as they alter. A small movement by you can make a big difference to the ease of an opponent's shot. Keep close to the post nearest to the player with the ball — the *near post*. This narrows the angle of the shot, and makes sure that the ball will have to pass in front of you.

- Above all, goalkeepers need the courage to face oncoming players without flinching.

Restarting play

When you or your team are to restart the play, make sure you gain full advantage from the situation. Here are some points to watch:

Throw-ins

Practise the technique of throwing in until you can make an accurate throw every time. Then practise some more to add power to the throw. A strong senior player should be able to throw from the corner flag to the goal-mouth. Don't simply think of distance, though — a short throw to a player who is well positioned may be of far more value.

Goal kicks

The rest of the team should know how far their goalkeeper can kick, bearing in mind that the distance will vary according to the strength and direction of the wind. Forwards need to be in the midfield area, ready to take up the attack if the goalkeeper can get the ball to them. Watch out for offside if you go past the halfway line.

Corners

A corner kick should always end up with a shot at goal. Try out different routines which you can bring into play when your side has a corner. Build variety into your approach: don't always boot the ball to the same player or to the same place in front of the goal.

The goalie puts the ball back into play with a goal kick.

Learn to make the best use of your team-mates in front of the goal. For example, if the ball is coming in from the right-hand corner, a left-footed kicker stands a slightly better chance of striking at goal than a right-footer.

A player cannot be offside directly from a corner kick, so if you are the first to play the ball after the kick has been taken, you can shoot and score even if there are not two defenders between you and the goal.

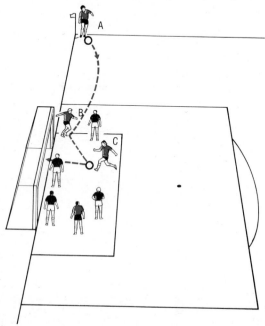

Figure 14 A successful corner-kick sequence: you cannot be offside directly from a corner kick, so B can receive the ball perfectly legally. A will need to be a left-footer to perform this corner kick successfully.

A corner kick leads to fierce action in the goal-mouth.

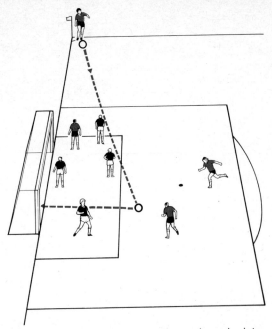

Figure 15 A corner kick across the goal can be intercepted by an incoming attacker with a good chance of scoring.

Indirect free kicks

Although you cannot score directly in this case, you can often turn a free kick into a scoring opportunity. Planning on the practice field is a great help here, and the techniques you use for corners can also work from some free kicks. Resist the temptation to boot the ball and hope for the best...

Penalty area puzzle
Indirect free kicks can be awarded within the penalty area. Defenders have to be ten yards (9.15 m) from the ball, so where do they go if the kick is given less than ten yards from the goal?

Answer: they have to stand on the goal-line.

Direct free kicks

This is a free kick after a deliberate foul, and you can score without another player having to touch the ball. You have to decide whether to take it very quickly, without preparation, or to take your time for a "set-piece" attack. If your team are well positioned and all in touch with the situation, you may wish to maintain the momentum of the attack and take the kick before the other side have re-grouped.

If you decide on the slower method, you can expect the other side to form a wall with their players in order to block a shot at goal. This is when practice at kicking a chip shot over the wall, or a curving shot around it, will pay off. If the player taking the kick hasn't got the skill to perform a shot of this type, it is far better to try a tight passing routine to get past the opposition. A short pass to the side will often give a clear shot at goal.

Figure 16 You can score from a set-piece direct free kick, if you have the skill to curve your shot around the "wall" of defensive players.

Penalty kicks

You rarely get a better chance to score than this, so practise taking penalties as often as you can against anyone you can persuade to go in goal. You will soon develop your own techniques for beating the goalkeeper, but if you are really short of ideas against an unknown goalie, remember that most people are right-handed, so you might improve your chances if you shoot to his left.

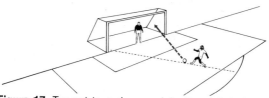

Figure 17 Try not to make your intentions obvious. Here the player taking the penalty runs up in line with the goalkeeper's right-hand post, but kicks the ball just inside the left-hand one.

A player's view of the penalty kick. Marc kicks up dust from the penalty spot, and seems to have beaten the goalkeeper this time.

7

Fitness for soccer

Football demands a special type of fitness and strength. It is no good developing wonderful skills with the ball if you are exhausted after ten minutes! During the one-and-a-half hours of a soccer match, the players will run for about five miles (eight kilometres), half at sprinting pace, half at a fast jog. This is not easy running, but a mixture of explosive sprints followed by abrupt stops, and repeated movements sideways and backwards, too.

Strength is an advantage; it helps you to resist shoulder charges and makes it harder for the strong players on the other side to dominate. Don't despair if you are not very tall, though: it is easier for a small, agile player to succeed than one who is strong but slow.

> Young players should not take part in strength training using weights. Until the bones are fully formed (usually by about age seventeen), there is a risk of permanent damage.

It is no good being a gifted player if you don't take the trouble to be fit. Unfit players cannot compensate for laziness by extra skill — they don't get the ball often enough! On pages 47–50 you will find some routines and exercises which will help you to keep fit. If you are a member of a well-organised football club, there should be a trainer or coach who will be able to help you with exercises which will build both speed and stamina. To benefit from these, you have to get into the habit of doing them *frequently* — every day if you can.

Fitness exercises and routines

Young players can keep acceptably fit by playing plenty of scratch games with their friends and not spending too much time sitting in front of the television. Children should also be helped to enjoy a sensibly balanced diet which will stop them getting overweight. As you grow and begin to take a serious interest in the game, fitness training becomes more and more important. There's no need to overdo it, though — keep a good balance of exercise and play: some parents and coaches forget that the object of the game is *enjoyment*, and that all training for youngsters should be designed with this in mind.

Here are some ideas for training routines which will give entertaining practice. The areas can be very simply marked out with cones or plastic tape. You can even use the old schoolyard favourite of a pile of coats to mark corners.

Spare corner
(for three players, using one ball)

Mark a square with sides up to 11 yards (10 metres) long. Each player stands at a corner. Any player starts, by passing to one of the others: *immediately* the ball has been passed, the player must run at full speed to the vacant corner. You can pass anywhere except back to the player who passed to you. Keep the action going *fast*.

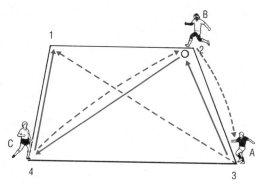

Figure 18 Spare corner: on this diagram the corners are labelled 1 to 4. A (at 3) kicks to B (at 2), and at once runs to 1, the spare corner. Now B (at 2) kicks to C (at 4), and runs to 3. C (at 4) kicks to A (at 1), and runs to 2. And so on... The game — which is much easier to play than to describe — can continue for as long as you like.

Note for coaches: Make the size of the square suit your players; 6 yards (5.5 metres) is enough for young children. Sixty seconds of intense play will do to start with, rising to ninety seconds for older players.

Shuttle sprints
(one player at a time, against the clock, or two or
more, as a race)

Set markers at 5, 10, 15, 20 and 25 yards (use metric
equivalents if you prefer) from a line. Run to the first
marker, return, run to the second marker, return, and so
on. This is much more tiring than it looks. Try complet-
ing the course three times to begin with, then gradually
build up until you can manage nine times at reasonable
speed without stopping.

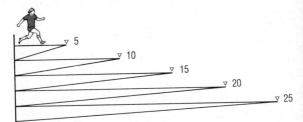

Figure 19 Shuttle sprints

> **Note for coaches:** You can vary this by making the
> players touch the ground with a hand at each marker.
> For dribbling practice, let the players try the shuttle
> sprint with a ball.

Duel to the line
(two players)

Two players stand back-to-back on a line. Each faces a
mark or flag ten yards away. On a signal, they sprint
around their mark, then around the other one, and back
to the line. The first home wins.

Figure 20 Duel to the line

> **Note for coaches:** This deceptively simple test is a lot
> more fun than it sounds. Try it!

The exercises described so far are very good for
developing sprinting and direction-changing. Distance-
running can be built up by using the following routines
around the pitch:

Fast and slow
(for the whole team)

Starting from one corner, run fast down one touchline; jog along the goal-line; run down the next touchline; jog to the starting point. Repeat several times.

Figure 21 Fast and slow

Note for coaches: Reverse the direction from time to time. The task becomes easier if you make the players run hard along the goal-line, giving them the length of the touchlines for the recovery jog. The exercise should not develop into a race.

Speed laps
(for the whole team)

Start at corner A, run fast around the pitch to B, then walk to A. Repeat.

Figure 22 Speed laps

Penalty shuttles
(for the whole team)

Start on the centre spot. Run to the penalty spot, then down the field to the other penalty spot, and finish with a jog back to the centre. A fresh player sets off as the previous one reaches the first penalty spot. Repeat.

Note for coaches: If you have enough helpers, you can have a ball on each penalty spot for the runners to try to score with.

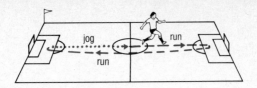

Figure 23 Penalty shuttles

Training exercises

Some simple exercises can help you to improve particular techniques: try this for strengthening your throw-in:

Throw-in tennis
(for two players)

The players stand a few yards each side of a set of goalposts, and throw the ball over the crossbar to each other. Each time the thrower takes one step backwards. The first to fail to clear the bar is the loser.

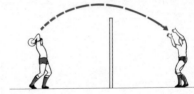

Figure 24 Throw-in tennis

Both sides shooting
(for five players)

This provides shooting practice, and also keeps the goalkeeper on the hop! Set up a goal about four yards wide, and place a marker about ten yards in front of the goal and another one ten yards behind it. Two players stand behind each marker, with the goalkeeper in the middle. Play starts when the goalie throws the ball to any player, who then has to pass or shoot. You are only allowed to shoot if you are behind your marker. If a shot is saved, the ball is thrown to the other pair of players, who are immediately in play. Shots which go wide are fair game for the opposite pair, who are allowed to come forward to gather them up.

> **Note for coaches:** If the players are quite experienced you can allow them to touch the ball once only. Less experienced players are allowed two touches.

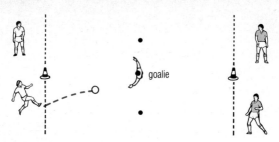

Figure 25 Both sides shooting

Goalkeeping practice

Goalkeepers need to have a natural aptitude for their job, but their effectiveness can be built up further by regular practice. A good way of encouraging goalkeepers to cover their goal-mouth at full stretch is by placing a spare ball in the centre of it. The goalkeeper has to dive over this ball to save shots which are made to the other side of it.

> **Note for coaches:** Most goalkeepers prefer to dive to a particular side: this practice can be used to help them improve on the other side.

This exercise encourages the goalkeeper to develop height and distance when he dives. He is not allowed to touch the ball on the goal-line.

Training games

Many variations of the full game can be devised for practice sessions. Generally the object is to keep all the players close to the ball and provide constant action. Apart from small-team games of five or six a side, played on a restricted playing area, try this practice for two teams which uses the whole pitch:

The playing area is divided down the middle as shown in Figure 26, and players have to stay on their own side. Two balls are used (it helps if they are of different colours), and play is continuous. Throw-ins are taken from the outside touchline only, and after a goal the ball is put back into play by the goalkeeper. Offside rules are relaxed. The periods of play need only be short — try ten minutes each way. You will find that action is fast, and there are plenty of opportunities to pass and score. The fact that there are two balls constantly in play keeps the goalkeepers occupied too!

Figure 26 Five-a-side times two: the goalies have to keep alert!

Note for coaches: This two-ball game is a good way of keeping a large training group occupied: concentrate on keeping play flowing — don't stop for minor infringements. The players rapidly pick up passing, positioning and shooting skills which will serve them immediately they play "real" soccer.

Injury

The physical demands of soccer can lead to all sorts of injury if you do not take sensible precautions. The first lesson to learn is the importance of warming-up properly before the match or training session, and warming-down again afterwards.

Unfortunately, many senior soccer players have developed the habit of dramatising incidents on the field in the hope that the referee will give a free kick or penalty. As a result we see a figure writhing on the ground, apparently close to death, who is running about at full speed a few minutes later. This gives a bad impression to young players in two ways: they imagine that serious injury really can be cured quickly, and they also come to accept that unsporting behaviour is a natural part of the game.

If you do suffer from a genuine injury of any type, get medical attention at the earliest opportunity. Don't play on regardless. However, when you get ordinary bumps and bruises, don't make a big deal of it — everyone on the soccer field gets them at some time or other.

Soft-tissue injuries

Even with very good warm-up routines and care in play, in a sport like soccer there will inevitably be some injuries to muscles, tendons and ligaments. If the injury appears at all serious, get proper medical attention at once. However, minor injuries can be given the "RICE" treatment:

Rest Stop using the injured part — if you don't rest it, permanent damage may result.

Ice Apply ice, through a plastic bag or cloth, to the injured area for 10 to 20 minutes. This will cause the blood vessels and tissues to contract, restricting the blood flow and reducing the swelling. Repeat every three hours if necessary.

Compression Keep swelling to a minimum by wrapping an elastic or crêpe bandage around the area. This can be placed over the ice-pack if necessary. Take care not to bind the bandage too tightly.

Elevation Raising the injured part will help excess fluid to drain from the damaged area, again reducing swelling.

In all cases, seek medical advice if there is no improvement within 48 hours.

8

Developing your skill

As you gain experience in any sport, your skills will naturally develop. This is particularly true of team games such as soccer, because the increasing standards of your team-mates and opponents put greater demands on your own abilities.

When you start, you will probably tend to think just of yourself and the opposite goal, and the positions of the other players will be little more than a blur! Soon their positions will become clearer, and you will realise that you have a job to do as part of a team. Now you can understand the core of the game:

- **control** the ball

- **pass** it on

- **support** the player in possession

If ever you find yourself becoming bogged down by technical details, remember that you are playing the game for fun, and get back to these basics. You will soon find that you are fitting into the team again.

Coaching schemes

In almost every country in the world there are schemes to help you to play better soccer. Some of these are local ones, organised quite informally by parents, youth groups or teachers. Others have backing by the football governing bodies and the support of international companies such as Coca-Cola. You will find that there are county or regional schemes which are usually graded according to age and ability. In almost every country there are professional coaches or organisers whose responsibility is to operate training schemes at all levels: don't be afraid to ask, and find out what is available. The simplest place to start is by enquiring at your local club.

Do join a scheme if you possibly can, and take part wholeheartedly. Your soccer skills will improve rapidly with regular tuition, but *you* must put the effort in.

The organisations listed on page 56 will be able to send you details of training schemes for young footballers.

Figure 27 Many areas have their own local coaching programmes. Here is some of the material from the Leeds City Council Football Development Scheme.

A hard game ends with a handshake.

Useful addresses

British Isles

The Football Association
16 Lancaster Gate
London
W2 3LW

The Scottish Football Association
6 Park Gardens
Glasgow
G3 7YE

The Irish Football Association
20 Windsor Avenue
Belfast
BT9 6EG

The Football Association of Wales
3 Westgate Street
Cardiff
CF1 1JF

The Football Association of Ireland
80 Merrion Square South
Dublin 2
Eire

Overseas

The Australia Soccer Federation
36–38 Clarence Street
Sydney
NSW 2000
Australia

The New Zealand Football
    Association
PO Box 18296
Glen Innes
Auckland
New Zealand

The Canadian Soccer Association
1600 James Naismith Drive
Gloucester
Ontario
K1B 5N4
Canada

The United States Soccer
    Federation
1750 East Boulder Street
Colorado Springs
CO 80909
USA

International

Fédération Internationale de Football Association (FIFA)
Case Postale 136
CH-8030 Zürich
Switzerland